Student Workbook
For
Making Conversation
Work for YOU

Includes

Conversation, Drama, Grammar, Games

FUN

Dr. Paul R. Friesen

iUniverse books may be ordered through booksellers or by contacting:

iUniverse
1663 Liberty Drive
Bloomington, IN 47403
www.iuniverse.com
1-800-Authors (1-800-288-4677)

ISBN: 978-1-4502-8247-5 (sc)
ISBN: 978-1-4502-8248-2 (ebook)

Printed in the United States of America

iUniverse rev. date: 12/14/2010

Table of Contents

Time

1. _hour_   2._____   3._____   4._____   5._____

6._____   7.__day__   8._____   9._____   10._____

11._____   12._____   13._____   14._____   15._____

16._____   17._____   18._____   19._____   20._____

21._____   22._____   23._____   24._____   25._____

Action

26._____   27._____   28.__watch_   29._____   30._____

31._____   32._____   33._____   34._____   35.__play__

36._____   37._____   38._____   39._____   40._____

41._____   42._____   43._____   44._____   45._____

46._____   47._____   48._____   49._____   50._____

Motion

51._____ 52._____ 53._____ 54._shopping 55._____

56._____ 57._____ 58._studying 59._____ 60._____

61._____ 62._____ 63._____ 64._____ 65._____

66._____ 67._____ 68._____ 69._____ 70._____

71._____ 72._____ 73._____ 74._____ 75._____

Emotion

76._____ 77._____ 78._____ 79._____ 80._____

81.___sad___ 82._____ 83._____ 84._____ 85._____

86._____ 87._____ 88._____ 89._miffed__ 90._____

91._____ 92._____ 93._____ 94._____ 95.__blue___

96._____ 97._____ 98._____ 99._____ 100._____

CR CR CR **Notes** CR CR CR

Flash video is available on DVD

Writing

Step 1

Choose one (1)

TIME/action/motion/emotion

word from the list.

Write them in the boxes.

EXAMPLE

❶ Hour/play/hitting/hard	❷

❸	❹

Step 2

Make a sentence with each of the four words.
Write them in the boxes below.
You can mix the order of the words to help you.

❶ At five o'clock I play baseball, hitting the ball hard.

❷

❸

❹

Step 3   Read them **out loud** in front of the class.

5

```
┌─────────────────┐
│        D        │
└─────────────────┘
```

Writing

┌──┐
│ Look at your 100 Words and choose **TIME** and **ACTION** words to │
│ make 5 sentences with **D** or **PAST TENSE**. │
└──┘

Example: day (time)   watch (action)
One <u>day</u> **I** <u>watched</u> **the birds at the park**.

1._____

2._____

3._____

4._____

5._____

_____

_____

Flash video is available on DVD

S

❋❋The letter **S** is used to tell me **WHO** is speaking.

Writing

Example – hour (time) watch (action)

He watches his children for hours.

1.____

2.____

3.____

4.____

5,____

6.____

7____

8.____

Flash video is available on DVD

Putting it all together

You have made 18 sentences. Put them all into a paragraph to describe the person sitting beside you.

My partner **HAS** a nice watch. He **PLAYS** computer games in his bedroom at night. He **PLAYED** a computer game last night.

_____

_____

_____

_____

_____

_____

Flash video is available on DVD

Step 3   The Dialogue

Use your sentences to create a dialogue. A dialogue is basically
QUESTION — ANSWER — QUESTION — ANSWER
Add an expression and you can have fun. Let's do it.
USE BODY LANGUAGE like waving your hands, etc.

Jake: Hey Sue! Did you see the new Professor yet?

Sue: No I haven't. What is he wearing?

Jake: Well, he has a nice watch. He is also wear ____ a green suit
jacket. He ____ blue hair and he is wear____ a purple tie.

Sue: Really? I have been in the Library all morning.
Maybe George has seen him.
Hey George! Have you seen the new Professor?

George: Yes. I think so. What is ____ wear____?

_____ : _____ .

_____ ?

_____ : _____ .

_____ ?

_____ : _____ .

_____ ?

_____ : _____ .

_____ ?

STEP 4   Keep Going

_____:

_____:

_____:

_____:

_____:

_____:

ADD MORE TO INCLUDE ALL STUDENTS IN THE CLASS.

Example --

1. An invitation to a party. You must invite a new person to it.

Me: Hi Joan. My friends are having a party would you like to come to it?

Answer I want ----

Enthusiastic ~~ **Joan**: Yes, I would love to come.
Where is it?

Polite refusal ~~ *No thanks!*
I have other appointments. Maybe another time!

2. You are wanting to find a date.
Answer I want ----

Enthusiastic

_____

Polite refusal

_____

3. You want to return a pair of pants but you need to find the right person.
Answer I want ----

Enthusiastic

_____

Polite refusal

_____

4. You want to talk to your boss about something personal.

        Answer I want ----

Enthusiastic

_____

Polite refusal

_____

5. You want to apologise to someone but they are busy.

        Answer I want ----

Enthusiastic

_____

Polite refusal

_____

6. You are traveling on the subway and you need to get out but there are too many people.

  Answer I want ----

Enthusiastic

_____

Polite refusal

_____

7. **Homework** — You must write down 2 situations when you needed an introduction and which words you used.

CIRCLE   (enthusiastic)   /   polite refusal

Situation -- _____

_____

Answer I wanted ---

_____

_____

Answer I received ---   enthusiastic   /   polite refusal

_____

Situation -- _____

_____

Answer I wanted ---

_____

_____

Answer I received ---   enthusiastic   /   polite refusal

_____

_____

What do I want to know?
What information do I want to ask about?

Sue — Well,

_____

Jake --

_____

Sue --

_____

Jake --

_____

Sue --

_____

Jake --

_____

Sue --

_____

Jake --

_____

PRACTICING THE RULES

Try filling in the _____ blanks

Samples --

I ____ _____ing English.   I **am study**ing English.

He is _____ing at the teacher.   He is **looki**ng at the teacher.

The teacher ___ _____ing the class.   The teacher **is teach**ing the class.

She _____ kimchi.   She **eats** kimchi.

෬ ෬ ෬ Try fixing the problems ෬ ෬ ෬

My brother is travels to America.
                    My brother **is** travel**ling** to America

My friend working on the weekend.
           _____.

She working at Galleria.
           _____.

Do you works at Burger King?
           _____.

Does you working tomorrow?
           _____.

Are you study English?
           _____.

EXERCISE YOUR LEARNING

Problem Sentences

I wanting lunch for pizza.
Where from your house?
I am shop for you.
Yesterday I will shop for books.
Tomorrow I had lunch with you.

What is NOT equal?
Time or Action and Why

Example --

1. Time is not equal with action. This is because the "ing" does not communicate the action. This communicates an incomplete idea.

2. _____
   _____

3. _____
   _____

4. _____
   _____

5. _____
   _____

Now rewrite the sentences to reflect how you would fix it. The sentence can be longer or shorter but must communicate a complete idea and the action and time MUST BE EQUAL.

Example --

       I want pizza for lunch today.

2. Where _____?

3. I _____.

4. Yesterday I_____.

5. Tomorrow I_____.

Your Turn

Step 1   Listen to your friends when they speak English.
            Or, Use your own sentences to do this exercise
            (not English speakers)

Step 2   Write 5 sentences that sound good to you.

Step 3   Fix them so that EVERYTHING is EQUAL.

COMMUNICATE with ACTION

-- act out instead of speak.

Choose twelve (12) action words from your list of 100 words and make an action for them.

1 ❋dance   2. _____   3. _____   4. _____

5. _____   6. _____   7. _____   8. _____

9. _____   10. _____   11. _____   12. _____

❋   Dance around a bit, close to your desk or in front of the class.
Have the class guess what the word is to add some fun to the
class activity.

-- put a sequence of words together.

Choose six (6) of these words and make 6 sentences.
Use the **Time/ Action or** Motion/ **Emotion** sequences.

1. **I   like   to dance   before I go to bed at night.**
   Emotion   Action   Time

2._____ .

3._____ .

4._____ .

5._____ .

6._____ .

-- communicate whole ideas **without speaking**.

Write your 6 sentences in a paragraph.
Then use **only** your body language to tell the class what you wrote.

_____

_____

_____

_____

_____

Write two conversation sequences of three ideas.

Thinking

1. What do I want to **know** in my conversation?

What do I want to talk or ask about? (topic)

1. a. Cars— fast, style, brand, color, drivers, car shows
b. _____
c. _____

2. What do I want the person to **hear** so I can get a good answer to my question?
What are good questions to ask?

2. a. What is your favourite car? / Do you like cars? / ___
b. _____
c. _____

Writing

Example --

Me: Hello, Sam. What is your ***schedule*** this weekend?

Sam: I have nothing planned this weekend. Why do you ask?

Me: Well, There is a car show in Seoul. Do you want to come with me?

Sam: Sounds great! What time is it?

Me: It starts at 2:00 on Saturday. Can you meet me at the COEX
Mall at 1 o'clock?

The answer is given and one more question?

Sam: Ok. I will meet you. See you Saturday at 2:00.

~~~ Make your own with B or C topics

Topic B -- _____

| Me: _____ |
| :_____ |
| Me: _____ |
| ____:_____ |
| Me: _____ |
| ____:_____ |
| Me:_____ |
| ____:_____ |

100 More Words

Think of 100 more words. These words will help you build the next part of your skills. It is harder but keeps working on this until all the word lines are filled.

Age

1 young   2_____   3_____   4_____   5_____

6_____   7_____   8_____   9_____   10 old

11_____12_____   13_____   14_____   15_____

16_____17_____   18_____   19_____   20_____

21_____22_____   23_____   24_____   25_____

Size

26_____   27_____   28_____   29 huge   30_____

31_____   32_____   33_____   34_____   35_____

36_____   37_____   38_____   39   tiny   40_____

41_____   42_____   43_____   44_____   45_____

46_____   47_____   48_____   49_____   50_____

Place

51 _____ 52 _____ 53 _____ 54 island 55 _____

56 _____ 57 _____ 58 _____ 59 _____ 60 _____

61 _____ 62 _____ 63 _____ 64 _____ 65 _____

66 _____ 67 coast 68 _____ 69 _____ 70 _____

71 _____ 72 _____ 73 _____ 74 _____ 75 _____

Color

76 _____ 77 _____ 78 _____ 79 _____ 80 _____

81 pink 82 _____ 83 _____ 84 _____ 85 _____

86 _____ 87 _____ 88 _____ 89 _____ 90 _____

91 pastel 92 _____ 93 _____ 94 _____ 95 _____

96 _____ 97 _____ 98 _____ 99 _____ 100 _____

The Low students should focus on concrete ideas.
The higher ones should learn vocabulary.

100 MORE WORDS

Step 1

Choose 1 word from each column.

age/ size/ place/ color

❶ young / huge / coast / pastel	❷
❸	❹
❺	❻
⑦	⑧

Step 2

Make a sentence with all four words.

❶ A **young** couple went to the **huge pastel coast**.

❷

❸

❹

❺

❻

⑦

⑧

Step 3

Choose 1 word from each of the **previous** 100 words sequence.
    time / action / motion / emotion

❶ hour / play / hitting / hard	❷
❸	❹

Step 4

Put all 8 words together.

time / action / motion / emotion / age / size / place / color

❶   hour / play / hitting / hard / young / huge / coast / pastel
❷
❸
❹

CR   CR   CR

Step 5

Now make sentences to fit these 8 words.

❶ At 5:00 p.m. young men play baseball on the huge pastel coast hitting the ball hard.

Time	age	action		size	color	place	motion	emotion

❷ _____

_____

❷ _____

_____

❷ _____

_____

Which communicates the best and why?

_____

_____

_____

ଔ   ଔ   ଔ

The Drama -- Where Am I?

Introduction to the Conversation

Me: Excuse me.
    Do you **have a minute**?

Sam: Yes?

Introduction to the Topic

Me: Where **am** I?

Sam: You are in Seoul! (Duh)

Continue the Topic

Me: I know that, but **where** in
    Seoul?

Sam: Ahh, this is Sadang-dong.

Me: I am looking for Dunkin Donuts.
    Do you know where it **is**?

Sam: I am sorry but I do not know.
    Maybe the security man would
    know.

Me:

_____

_____

There is a problem with this conversation.
Where is it?

_____

List the **time** words
_minute_____

_____

List the **action** words
_know_____

_____

List the **motion** words
_looking_____

_____

List the **emotion** words
_Ahhh_____

_____

_____

The Situation - Where Am I?

Situation — You are looking for a shoe store called Suzy Q's. You need to ask someone for help in Saskatoon.

Choose a good question from "Good Questions" in this chapter and
fill in the lines with your drama.

Example –

Introduction

1. **Me***:* Excuse me. Do you **have a minute**?

----- This is a polite way to intrude on someone's time or space.

   2. **Me***:* Excuse me. Do you **have a minute**? **I am lost** and need to find Suzy Q's Shoe Store. Can you help me?

Response

1. **Sam***: I am sorry I'm busy.*
        (no response. Sam continues walking without speaking)

2. **Sam***: Sure! Suzy Q's is one block over.*
      : I'm sorry I don't know where the shoe store is. Maybe you can ask at the gas station on the corner.

   3. **Sam***: (no response. Sam continues walking without speaking)*

Sam with map*: Well, you are here on the map and you want to go there. It's not too hard to find.*

Continue the Topic

Me: _____

_____

Sam:

_____

_____

Me:

_____

_____

Sam: _____

_____

Me:

_____

_____

Sam: _____

_____

Me: _____

_____

Sam: _____

_____

Situation 2 - Where Am I?

You must ❶ *introduce yourself*.

Then you must ❷ *introduce your problem* (topic).

Finally you must move to find it.

❸ *Finish the Conversation.*

ೞ ೞ ೞ ೞ ೞ ೞ

Situation

❶ I want to ask if a Store has a special item I want to buy.

Good Questions

❶ _____ **?**

❷ _____ **?**

❸ _____ **?**

Conversation

Me: _____

Sam: _____

Me: _____

Sam: _____

Me: _____

Sam: _____

❷ REVERSE THE SITUATION

I want to ask someone if I can help them because *THEY* look lost.

<u>Good Questions</u>

❶ _____ ?

❷ _____ ?

❸ _____ ?

Example --

Me: Good morning. You look a bit lost, may I help you?

Sam: Ahhh.. yes! I am looking for a Burger King. Is there one around here?

Me: _____

Sam: _____

Me: _____

Sam: _____

❸ SITUATION

I just want to ask if you have time for coffee to chat.

What would I talk about? (Topics)

How would I introduce the topic I want to chat about?

TOPICS

1. _____

2. _____

3. _____

GOOD QUESTIONS

1. _____

2. _____

3. _____

INTRODUCTIONS

1. _____

2. _____

3. _____

Ը   Ը   Ը

A conversation with **more** than two people
1+1+__ =?

Many times you meet someone but you can't get past hello. You didn't memorize enough or you didn't develop your skill enough.

Practice this together and then in groups of three.

Hello: How U doin'?
  Me 2: Great and you?
Hello: My name is Hello! What's yours?
  Me 2: Me 2.
Hello: Really?
  Me 2: Yes, and this is my friend Really.
Really: Nice to meet you. Really.
  Hello: Me 2. What are you doing today with Really?
Me 2: Well, I would like to go for coffee.
  Hello: Really. How about you?
Really: Well, I will just follow Me 2.

Sounds silly I know.

What is the problem with this conversation?

Are there any new phrases?

REVIEW

The sequence

Make a question (Q) — answer the question (A) —

What does the third person do or say?

Question — Answer — **?** — Question — Answer — **?**

LET US GET STARTED

Situation – Two friends are meeting at Square Bucks Coffee. One friend is bringing a friend who does NOT know the other.

Square Bucks Coffee Shop

S1: Hello. Q – Sam! Who did you bring with you?

S2: A -- Hi John! This is my friend Sue. Sue this is my friend John.

S1: Hi Sue! Q -- _____

ભ   ભ   ભ

How many different good questions can we think about to ask Sue in the dialogue above?

1. _____

2. _____

3. _____

4. _____

5. _____

_____

_____

_____

_____

> Many times you meet someone but they or you have a friend.
>
> How you introduce or ask about this friend is important.

Example --
Asking about their friend

❶ Who is he/she?
  or
❶ Who is your friend?

❷ What does your friend do?

Introducing your friend

❶ This is my friend ____.
  or
❶ This is ____ my friend.
  or
❶ I'd like you to meet my friend. ____ this is John.

Example --   Q = question   A = answer

S1: Hello. Q – Sam! Who did you bring with you? ❶

S2: A -- Hi John! This is my friend Sue. ❶
                Sue this is my friend John. ❶

S1: Hi Sue! Q -- What does your friend do? ❷

LET US CONTINUE THE CONVERSATION

Discussion

Which ones do you use most in your own language or culture?

_____

How does this compare with how you use English?

_____

How often do you have to introduce your friend to someone else?

_____

S1: Hello. Q – Sam! Who did you bring with you?

S2: A -- Hi John! This is my friend Sue. Sue this is my friend John.

S1: Hi Sue, Q -- What does your friend do?

S3: I am an Executive Assistant at Kwando Motors.
Q – How long have you known Sam?

S1: A - _____ Q—

_____

_____

_____

Be Aware of HOW you say things

Let's introduce your friend first

You are introducing your friend
   To another person in your social group.

-- A Social group is a group of people you hang out or socialize with.

You — Hey Bob!
   Bob!
   Bob.   This is *John*,   my friend   from <u>School</u>.
           This is *John*   a   buddy   from <u>Work</u>.
           This is *John*   a Business Associate
           This is *John*   an old friend   from my <u>home town</u>.

Who you are talking with?	*Who* you are *Introducing?*	What **relationship** they are to you?	What **connection** they are to the situation?

Let's Ask about Your Friend's friend

You — Hey Bob!
   Bob!
   Bob! Who is your friend?
                      (best)
        Is that someone from work/ your office?
                      (a bit rude)
        What's your friend's name?
                      (polite)
        Who is that person with you?
                      (if the person is not beside - **polite**)
        Who did you bring with you?
                      (just information not interest)

 C3   C3   C3

You Try It

Write four (4) situations that <u>you have</u>, or <u>think you will find yourself in</u> to introduce yourself to another person who is with a person you know.

1. _____

2. _____

3. _____

4. _____

Situation -- 1

You are bringing your friend to meet another.

Me: _____

Sue: _____

Friend: _____

_____ : _____

_____ : _____

_____ : _____

_____ : _____

CR   CR   CR

Situation -- 2

You are meeting your friend who has a surprise friend.

Me:

_____

Sue:

_____

Friend:

_____

_____:

_____

_____:

_____

_____:

_____

Situation -- 3

_____

Me:

_____

Sue:

_____

Friend:
_____ :

___:
_____

___:
_____

___:
_____

___:
_____

___:
_____

___:
_____

___:
_____

___:
_____

___:
_____

STEAK AND POTATOES

Steak words are the key focus of a full sentence.

Write down some words. They need to be 4 or 5 letters long. They should be nouns or topic words.

Steak words

1 soccer   2 _____   3 _____   4 _____

5 _____   6 _____   7 _____   8 _____

Potato words

— These are words that add to the idea. They are important and may be used as an object of a sentence.

These are NOT adjectives.

1 _____   2 ball_____   3 _____   4 _____

5 _____   6 _____   7 _____   8 _____

LET US CONTINUE THE MEAL

Write down some words to help the Steak and Potatoes.

I call these GARNISH. They are small words which help the other words work together.

Garnish words

1 ___like___ 2 _____ 3 ___a___ 4 _____

5 _____ 6 ___blue___ 7 _____ 8 _____

9 _____ 10 _____ 11 _____ 12 _____

13 _____ 14 _____ 15 _____ 16 ___the___

Put it together

Step 1

Write your words down.

Example --

Steak = soccer
Potato = ball
Garnish = like, blue, the

Step 2

Put them in a line.

Does this make sense? OF COURSE NOT.

Are there enough words to make sense? Maybe!

Do we need to add words or change words? Yes / No

Change words?

Which words would you change?

the **Steak**   the **Potato**   or   the **Garnish**?

Why would you change it or them?

_____

_____

Add words?

Which words would you add?

more **Potato**   or   more **Garnish**?

Why would you add it or them?

_____

_____

Finishing the idea

DIFFERENT COMBINATIONS

SAMPLE WORDS LIST — *Soccer ball like blue the.*

Step 3

Add some action with another potato word.

The blue like soccer ball was kicked by me.

Steak		Action + Time	Garnish + Potato

Now you have a good sentence that has all the elements of good communication.

Your turn to do some

Now you have better understanding of the idea you may want to change them. Look at your STEAK, POTATO, and GARNISH words. Do you want to change any now?

Change them now.

Step 4

Take one ❶ STEAK word + two ❷ Potato words + three ❸ GARNISH words and put them in a line.

_____ _____ _____ _____ _____ _____
  ❶   ❷   ❷   ❸   ❸   ❸

Now change them into a reasonable idea.

_____ _____ _____ _____ _____ _____

Now add words to finish the idea like **Step 3**

_____ _____ _____ _____ _____ _____

_____ _____ _____ _____

How does it look? *Do this again, on a separate page, for good practice.*

USE ALL THE WORDS YOU WROTE IN THE THREE CATEGORIES

℘   ℘   ℘

Real Practice

Use the sentences you have made to make a conversation. Do this in a team so you can communicate your ideas in a conversation format.

Example --
    --- The sentence we made ---

The blue like soccer ball was kicked by me.

Abe: Hello John!
John: Hello Abe! How are you doing?

Abe: I am doing ok. How about you?
John: Well,, I am in a little bit of trouble.

Abe: How come?
John: well, I was playing with a friend in the park and a soccer ball
        broke a car window.

Abe: Really?

John: Yes. They said that I have to pay for the window. It was the color of the ball that we were playing with that was the problem.

Abe: How terrible!

John: Yes! **The blue like soccer ball was kicked by me,** but it was not our ball. I feel terrible. My mother will be very angry.

Add a couple more

Abe:

_____

_____

John:

_____

Abe:

_____

John:

_____

CR   CR   CR

Time Travel
A point in time makes your English climb.

Refer to the first 100 word list you did before.

What words can be used to help understand time?

Thinking

When do you _____?

What **time** do you _____?

Tell me a time when _____

How **often** _____?

I study **from** _____ to _____

I ma**de** _____

I **am** dri**ving** _____

_____

Let's check it out.

Example --

There is a barbeque.

What information is missing?

What information do you need to know to understand what I want to tell you?

Write your answer as a QUESTION.

A. _____?

B. _____?

ಇ   ಇ   ಇ

Adding Time

Mark on a calendar these two dates, <u>*Sunday and July 4th*</u>.

Now, later, soon, never, sometime, future, past, week, weekend, day (Sunday….), o'clock, minute (s), seconds, hour (s), a.m., p.m., afternoon, morning, evening, night, noon, then, as soon as, for the time being, schedule, routine, continue, _____,

_____, _____

Make this connection so you can learn words that go together.

Now   --- I am + ____ing, is, make, give to,

Past   ---   _____

Future   ---   _____

After   ---   _____, _____, _____

Before --- _____, _____, _____

Communicating Time

Learning to use words together

Choosing the Topic

What topics do you want to talk about in your introduction?

❶ _____   ❷ _____

| Topic ❶ _____ |

What questions can you ask about this topic? Write five (5) questions.

1._____?

2._____?

3._____?

4._____?

5._____?

| Topic ❷ _____ |

What questions can you ask about this topic? Write five (5) questions.

1._____?

2._____?

3._____?

4._____?

5._____?

ᗩ   ᗩ   ᗩ

Step 1

Add the questions and then give answers in the following conversation.

Step 2

Underline the TIME words. Use the next page to finish the conversation.

Step 3

Me: Hello! How are you doing today?

    You: I'm doing great! What are you doing this weekend?

Me: I'm going to go fishing on Saturday? What about you

    You: Well, I think I will go to a movie Saturday night.

_____

_____

_____

_____

_____

_____

_____

_____

_____

_____

છ છ છ

A Point in Time

Rule # 1

Of conversation is that you must have a question and answer rhythm.

DO = ACTION

What do you **do** <u>on</u> holidays?

What do you **do** <u>*in*</u> your **free time**?

Rule # 2

What you want the <u>*other person to hear*</u> **you** stress.

Do + time

Now do it again with the "do" words changing places. Which one is better and easier to hear and understand? ❶ **or** ❷

❶ **or** ❷

❶ What **do** you do <u>**on**</u> holidays?

❷ What do you **do** <u>on</u> holidays?

❶ What **do** you do <u>in </u> your **free time**?

❷ What do you **do** <u>*in your*</u> **free time**?

Write a few of your own sentences using DO + ON.

_____

_____

_____

_____

☙ ☙ ☙

IN - - - - - - - SPACE, A PLACE, OR TIME

Each set of points is an "in" idea.

Make one sentence or question with "in".

LET'S TRY IT

. Hello! What are you doing **in** the mall?

    . I was shopping **in** the shoe store. What are you doing?

. Well! I am **in** the classroom looking for my books. Can you come help
    me?

    . I don't know. I don't think I can make it **in** time.

. How about **in** July? Would you have time then?

    . Yes, **in** July is better.

Make a conversation
    — ❶   choose a topic to ask about
      ❷   reply with "in".

_____

_____

_____

_____

_____

Think about the holidays in your Country.

How many can you list with their dates?

Use **on** and **in** to help you tell about **time**.

EXAMPLE — July 1 — Canada Day

On July 1 celebrate Canada Day. **In** the morning I sing "O Canada" and **in** the afternoon we dance **in** the street. **In** the evening some people drink Red Beer. I hope this year it is **on** a Friday.

On = a BIG BOX   In = a TIME BOX

ભ   ભ   ભ

Rewrite the paragraph and <u>three 3 "*at*" time phrases</u>. Remember "at" is a point in time. Morning, Friday, July 1, and other words communicate time but are big and not precise. Use "at" to communicate a very small point in time.

On July _____

_____

_____

_____

_____

Review Writing

Step 1

List the holidays or special days in one year.
Give their dates (time)

Name	Date

Example --

New Years Day   **On** January 1 (USA)

_____

_____

_____

_____

_____

_____

_____

_____

Adding Action

What **you** DO that is special **(action)**

Now add the words at / on / in to complete the sentence. Then make your own.

July 1/ Canada Day / Sing O Canada/ Dance in the Street/ Drink Red Beer

_____

_____

Adding Emotions

What **emotions** do you have on these special days?

Sad/ Happy/Excited/ .....

_____

_____

Step 2

Write a paragraph about this special day using the words you have learned.

Example --

On July 1, I <u>sing</u> "O Canada", <u>drink</u> red beer, and <u>dance</u> in the street. In the evening I <u>watch</u> the fireworks in the sky. I feel <u>happy</u> for my country. I feel <u>sad</u> because of the economy. I feel <u>excited</u> because it is a holiday for me.

_____

_____

_____

<u>Read this to the class or a friend when you are finished.</u>

Better Vocabulary
Better Communication

Remember the vocabulary on emotional value. The more vocabulary you can learn with these values, the **Better** your communication.

Vocabulary Challenge

Write your **action words** on one line and add (+) words that have the **same action**.

Example --

Sing = chant, yell   _____ _____ _____ _____

Dance = jump, swing, shuffle _____ _____ _____ _____

Drink = guzzle, sip, gulp   _____ _____ _____ _____

Watch = _____ _____ _____ _____

Write your **emotion words** on one line and add (+) words that have the same **emotion value**.

Example --

Sad = remorseful, unhappy   _____ _____ _____ _____

Happy = energetic, jovial   _____ _____ _____ _____

Excited = exuberant, giggly, nervous   _____ _____ _____ _____

_____ = _____ _____ _____ _____

ભ ભ ભ

Step 3

Fill in the blanks with **different** *words.*

On July 1, I _____ "O Canada", _____ red beer, and _____ in the street. In the evening I _____ the fireworks in the sky. I feel _____ for my country. I feel _____ because of the economy. I feel _____ because it is a holiday for me.

Write a paragraph using the **Time, Action, and Emotion** words. Use as many as possible.

_____

_____

_____

_____

_____

One more time with a different day.

_____

_____

_____

DISCUSSION

Do these extra words help you communicate better? Why?

Do these words help your writing, speaking, or both?

How do they help you?

Give some examples of how the words can <u>help</u> or <u>hinder</u> your **writing or speaking.**

_____

Small **WORDS COUNT**

Action / Motion

From — **POSITION** — start point of action
        (Action)

Inside — **POSITION** — **CLOSE**
       (Motion — you move something from outside to inside)

Toward — **DIRECTION** — **CLOSE**
       (Motion — you move something closer to an object)

Let's Try It Together

Around — _____ — _____ (_____)

Across — _____ — _____ (_____)

Beneath — _____ — _____ (_____)

By means of — _____ — _____ (_____)

Except for — _____ — _____ (_____)

Apart from — _____ — _____ (_____)

Concerning — _____ — _____ (_____)

With — _____ — _____ (_____)

Was this difficult? If it was you are very normal. Isn't that exciting?

When you learn to think of these small words as more than just words,
BUT IMPORTANT COMMUNICATION POINTS,
             YOU WILL COMMUNICATE BETTER.

ՅՅ   ՅՅ   ՅՅ

Small **Words** = **Big Communication**

The Almost Complete List of Small Words

About *above* according to *after* against *along* along with among *as* **as for** *at* because of *before* behind *below* beside *between* beyond **but*** by *despite* down *during* except *excepting* for *in* in addition **to** *in back of* in case of *in front of* in place of *in spite of* into *like* near *next of* off on *onto* on top of *out* out of *outside* over *past* regarding *round* **since** *through* throughout *till* to *under* underneath *unlike* until *up* upon *up to* within *without*

ℂℛ ℂℛ ℂℛ

Let's Try It Together

--- Use 4 ~ 5 small words plus to make a story or paragraph. Remember some small words need partner words like of, for, or in to communicate better.

Small words to use — _____

Sentence _____

_____

_____

_____

NOTE:

"Of" used together with other words = motion

"To" used together with other words = action **of object**

❋ ❋   Use the *Let's Try It Together* words to make them into sentences using

the same values.

_____

_____

_____

_____

_____

_____

_____

_____

_____

_____

The Small words Drama

Use the sentences you have just made and make a conversation with them.

Topic — Study English

Good Questions?

1. Why_____?

2. How _____?

3. When _____?

4. Where_____?

5. What _____?

Introduction

Me: Hello Sam! How are you doing today?
   Sam: I'm going ok. How about you?

Me: Well! English is hard for me. How is the English class for you Sue?
   Sue: I think it is hard, but it is also a lot of fun. The games are not so hard.
   Sam: You are right. But it is still hard for me. I am so busy.

(Use your questions and answers to finish the conversation)

Play the game

THE SMALL WORDS DRAMA GAME   ✳✳

Write the sentences used in the game on this page.

Sam: You are right. But it is still hard for me. I am so busy.

_____: _____

_____: _____

_____: _____

_____: _____

_____: _____

_____: _____

_____: _____

_____: _____

_____: _____

_____: _____

_____: _____

_____: _____

_____: _____

If you need more add more paper until you finish the game.
✳✳ **The game board and die are in the full version of this book. You can buy it online at any good bookstore, or ask your teacher.**

5 by 5 — Writing Plan

Step 1 — Plan for a topic you can talk about.

Step 2 — List 5 things about the topic

    1. _____
    2. _____
    3. _____
    4. _____
    5. _____

Step 3 — Think of 5 good questions for *each idea.*

Example — Cars — brand

Which _____?

What _____?

Why _____?

How did _____?

When _____?

Step 4 - Write an answer to the five questions **in a complete sentence**.

1.Q _____?

Answer -- _____

What is a good NEXT question which is **natural** in your thinking?

2. _____?

Answer — Because _____

3._____?

Answer

_____.

4. _____?

Answer

_____.

5. _____?

 Answer _____.

Continue with this until **all the 5 topics + 5 questions have 5 answers.**

Step 5 — Write **an introduction to the topic**.

_____

_____

_____

_____

_____

_____

ℭ℈ ℭ℈ ℭ℈

Let's Try Making an Essay

TOPIC — CARS

INTRODUCTION --

Cars! They are very exciting sometimes and come out with new styles and colours every year. I collect toy cars and make them with my Lego blocks. I like the BMW the best. It is a world famous brand and very fast.

Work ~~ Make some topics and follow the steps to make a good introduction.

Topic _____

Introduction

_____

_____

_____

_____

_____

_____

ଔ   ଔ   ଔ

About Transitions

What are some that we use a lot in our writing and speaking for comparisons?

But = positive to negative

    However = *more to think about*

        Therefore = <u>*to finish the idea*</u>

Some others that show time are ~~

Then = *After A then B*
Whenever = at anytime + first action

Here are some others that show time ~ Memorize them

After   before   currently   during   soon   eventually

finally   first, second... etc.   formerly   immediately   previously

initially   lastly   later   meanwhile   next   simultaneously

        CR   CR   CR

Using the Transitions

What's next?

Use transitions to finish a previous conversation **about cars**.

Or

Change the topic **to one you like by using transition words or questions**.

Or

Finish the Essay **that you started on the previous pages**.

_____

_____

_____

_____

_____

_____

_____

_____

CR   CR   CR

5 x 5   Expanded

Outlining

~~ Making an outline **helps writing become faster**.

~~ Making an outline makes **finding problems faster and easier**.

~~ Making an outline helps us **think better in a conversation**.

Choose your Topic _____

I. Idea (ONE WORD)_____

A. About the topic — **focus on about the one word** — use Time or
    transition to start is good. _____

B. _____

C. _____

D. _____

E. _____

II. Idea (ONE WORD) _____

A. About the topic — **focus on about the one word**
                    — use Time or transition to start is good.

B. _____

C. _____

D. _____

E. _____

III. Idea (ONE WORD) _____

A. About the topic — **focus on about the one word**
    — use Time or transition to start is good.

B. _____

C. _____

D. _____

E. _____

IV. Idea (ONE WORD) _____

A. About the topic — **focus on about the one word**
    — use Time or transition to start is good.

B. _____

C. _____

D. _____

E. _____

The Essay

An essay has three parts
        Introduction — Body — Conclusion

ত্ত   ত্ত   ত্ত

The Conversation

A conversation works best in a question/answer format.

Find a partner or two and make a conversation using the sentences you have made.

You will have to CHANGE or ADD questions to make this work.

Put in the small words and transitions to help make this conversation.

Change topics at least once per person.

Do this on a separate paper or file and make it as long as possible.

ত্ত   ত্ত   ত্ত

Final Activity

Who would you like to talk with about this topic?
Anybody -- Teacher -- Close friend -- etc.

CHOOSING THE RIGHT PERSON GIVES YOU THE BEST CONVERSATION. YOU CHOOSE A TOPIC FOR THE PERSON YOU WANT TO TALK WITH. THIS MAKES TALKING EASIER AND MORE COMFORTABLE.

Can I change the topic so I am more comfortable?

PREPARE AND LEARN TRANSITIONS SO YOU CAN CHANGE THE TOPIC IF YOU ARE ASKED A QUESTION YOU DO NOT LIKE.

How do I stop the conversation or exit it?

STOPPING A CONVERSATION IS NOT SO HARD. ALL YOU HAVE TO DO IS NOT ASK A QUESTION. IF YOU JUST SAY YES AND NO AND THE CONVERSATION WILL STOP NATURALLY.

As a final Activity we will start with one person.

The first person will choose a topic to start.

This first person will choose another student to have a conversation with.

This conversation will continue with five questions or ideas from the topic.

Then the second person will choose a third person and continue or change the topic using a transition.

The first person can sit down and watch.
This will continue until all the students have had a chance.

I hope you have had Fun.

ଓ୨   ଓ୨   ଓ୨

Final Thoughts for A brighter future

Thinking

What topics do I like to talk about?

CHOOSING TOPICS YOU LIKE TO CHAT ABOUT MAKES IT EASIER TO BEGIN AND CONTROL A CONVERSATION.

What topic would you like to talk about?

CHOOSE ONE OR TWO TOPICS TO EXPAND ON. TRYING TO TALK ABOUT TOO MANY THINGS IS CONFUSING AND FRUSTRATING.

IF YOU GET CONFUSED REMEMBER IT IS THE QUESTIONS THAT HELP YOU.

ASK A LOT OF QUESTIONS TO HELP YOU GET BACK TO THE TOPIC YOU WANT TO TALK ABOUT.

Why do I want to talk about it?

DO YOU WANT INFORMATION? DO YOU WANT TO DEVELOP A COMMON INTEREST?

When is a good time to talk about it?

One-one, group, quiet, noisy, night club, over coffee, etc.

Weekend Adventures
of
John and Sally

A
100 question
Conversation template
to develop skills
in the area
of
Topic development
in
conversation

Dr. Paul R. Friesen
2010

The Challenge

The challenge in any class is to help the student retain what they learn over a longer period of time. In Conversation class most books offer short conversations, which is good. In real life many of our conversations are with friends. In a job they are focused on ideas based on products we service or sell. The challenge is to have students develop skills to be active participants in conversations that are neither work nor friend related.

The Theory

The theory behind the 100 question format is to think longer about a focus topic. Each topic in the book has ideas to draw from. Each chapter has a focus topic. By writing a series of question – answer – question ideas they can develop a continuous flow in any conversation. After the initial series they will add things like; commands, time words, tenses, etc. They can develop a vocabulary using the books focus topic vocabulary. Using the ideas and vocabulary in a series of QAQ's they will begin to understand the nature and strategy of conversation, not just as rote memory, but as a living organism which can be manipulated to achieve purpose or information gathering.

The Purpose of the template

Because this is a new idea to the student, I wrote a week by week template which they could follow. There are 10 QAQ's in each chapter plus inserted ideas which are numbered. The goal was to achieve a 100 question conversation, through a 10 week 10 QAQ per week grid.

Will they be able to do it? My goal was not to achieve perfect grammar. It was to teach the pattern of conversation which, when learned would give a higher confidence to the student to participate in conversations where they may not otherwise feel compelled to enter.

I think that after studying several years of English, they have it in their head. Through hard work and a better understanding of conversation strategies they can take the conversation book, they have written with their peers to review at any time. Language changes, but the pattern does not very often.

I applaud the effort of all my students who have worked hard to do this. To put together a story line over 10 weeks is not easy. To do it with a student partner whom they have just met in class is even harder. But they have or will have done it. This is the template I made as their teacher to guide them.

For those who read this. I hope you can enjoy and use it in your class in whole or in part as a template for your students or for your self development in conversation

Preface

After 10 years of teaching there are some things you should figure out. The first is that changing the system through complaining is not effective. Second, if you are serious about teaching, and not just making money, the issues in the classroom and the system need to be explored so a solution can be developed. There are too many teachers who feel locked in the system. Even harder is to teach when the purpose of education is determined by how the image of the owner is kept and how much money can be made.

Education for profit does 2 things. The first is it often extends the material so long that it is most ineffective. The second is that when money, or the happiness of the student is foremost in the design, without well prepared teachers the system will breakdown. This is not only for Korea but for any system which is driven by greed and conformity.

The writers of large publishing companies have done an injustice in the area of conversation. They have ignored both the classroom and the culture issues. Therefore most, but not all (just a large majority), of all the ESL books designed for Conversation do not do an effective job of building the students capacity to continue a conversation. There are great games and ideas in each book. The grammar is important but the ideas are not built into one another. Each chapter is a standalone idea. The conversations too short and the activities fun but forgotten after the class is finished.

How to build better and longer conversations

To this end I challenged myself to develop a system which could be used to build several things. First it is to help the student understand the nature and structure of conversation. In this system I have used the Question – Answer – Question idea. It may seem very basic but in real life conversations are not continued for two basic reasons. The first is that what comes next is lost in the nervous tension of speaking. The second comes from a lack of ideas generated from topics talked about. Questions are the controlling part of a conversation. Therefore it would make logical sense to focus on this sequence first.

The second area of development is vocabulary. In this conversation you will find that there are 10 vocabulary words. Building vocabulary is not so hard. I would suggest the students learn to use a thesaurus. This is because they will learn words associated with the same ideas. Dictionaries are good but they often confuse the student, because they offer just definitions which cross-language creates a lot of communication problems.

A third, but very minor part is grammar. Grammar is important and as you learn new vocabulary the grammar will change. This link is vital to understanding the nature of conversation. We must remember what is ok in colloquial English is not always good grammar. In teaching conversation we must stay focused on effective communication leaving the cat to wag the tail, not the tail wag the cat.

Using this template you can manipulate what you want and expand the conversation every week. It has numbers to help you, and underlined idea and words which are associated with the topic. We shouldn't ignore the books that are in the market presently. We do need to consider ideas that fill the gap between the educational culture system and the current Korean system. The issue of efficacy is twofold. The first is that most books are written for intake into an English culture. Therefore the relevance and connection is assumed. In a monoculture this connection needs to be built in.

In the area of public and/or private school teaching the problem is that the American books used or suggested are not connected in topic to the rest of the curriculum. Bringing this together will give support to what is being taught. This in turn will motivate the student to learn as it is intertwined with the English being taught.

The purpose of this conversation template is to help bridge the gap for the teacher. I have found, in the University level that the creativity in topic development in disciplined writing and interaction reinforced other areas of focus in other classes taken by the students.

English conversation should not be taught as an anomaly to the curriculum, but together with it as foundational reinforcement to what is being taught in other classes in any language.

Examples from the template –

John: It's raining again. I hate rain. Oh hi! I was just speaking out loud. My name is John. I am a student. Do you live around here?[1]

Sally: No! I am new here. I don't like rain either. I'm a student at _____. I haven't seen you before. I'm Sally. Where do you go to school?

John: I go to _____ too. I am majoring in _____. What do you like to do on weekends?[2]

Sally: I look on the internet for movies and concerts. What do you like to do?
Medicine has a lot of homework.

Note— This is from the Introductions chapter. Notice that the standard greeting is left to follow a statement.

John: It's raining again. I hate rain. Oh hi! I was just speaking out loud. My name is John. I am a student. Do you live around here?[1]

Teaching students to break the ice before greeting provides a better cultural introduction. Blurting, or yelling out "Hi! How are you!" is truly ignorant in today's world. Teaching students to use better etiquette in any culture is important.

Using this initial statement, have the students create their own break- the - ice introductions, followed by a statement of their name. Expanding this idea to use first names for same age people and respectful names for older people will help with etiquette.

Notice that John does not ask for Sally's name. He asks a question that is nonintrusive and is generic in information. Do you live around here?[1]

The "1" is the beginning of the question – answer – question sequence. Asking for information is both polite and helps set the conversation on a topic to continue. Have the students write a list of 5 information questions that they can use as conversation starters. In a smaller class, where speaking activity is easily attained talk about the ideas and write them on the board. If speaking confidence is lacking writing them down will help them start.

Now you have started a conversation which is both polite in beginning, allowing the other person to refuse to join if they want, and a question to start if the other person is willing to join. Sally: No! I am new here. I don't like rain either. I'm a student at _____ . I haven't seen you before. I'm Sally. <u>Where</u> do you go to school?

Sally answers the "DO" question with a "No!" and then adds to the first statement. "Do" questions should receive a standard yes/no answer. This would apply often with "Are you...?", or the verb "to be" as well.

To continue the conversation Sally needs to add something and she responds to the first statement about rain. Rain is the common point of connection. Choosing a point of connection makes conversation easy and smooth. If there is no common point the other person's attention will not follow the direction of the conversation and it will die out quickly.

Sally follows the comment about rain with information that is equal to the information given to her by John. This is important because you need to listen to the information given. Now you have the question – answer and need to finish the sequence, asking the second question.

After a second remark about their relationship, " <u>I haven't seen you before</u>.", Sally gives her name and asks the second question to continue the conversation. <u>Where</u> do you go to school? This question will lead the conversation on the same topic as the first. Now the conversation has started. What is next? More of the same sequences with different questions. In the template you will find 10 sequences on the same topic. There will also be 10 vocabulary words that focus on the topic.

In this conversation John answers the question and adds more information. By adding more information the conversation is easier to continue. Without information your conversation will not be focused. When there is no focus you need to change the topic by asking a new topic question.

In this conversation John decides to change the conversation topic by asking a new question that will give new information. <u>What</u> do you like to <u>do</u> on weekends?[2] This is the first question of the new topic and a new sequence.

Learning to listen to important ideas you can delete the words that are not important to communication. <u>What</u> do you like to <u>do</u> on weekends? This allows you to listen to the idea better. "What" asks for a thing not a person or movement. "Like" sets the emotion as positive and enjoyable. "Do" is important because it asks the listener to respond with an action statement. It is linked to "What". "Do" at the beginning of the question, requires a yes/no answer. "Do" in the middle of the question requires a response that includes an action. "Weekends" sets the time of the action you are asking about.

Write various questions that you can ask that will give you information about a topic, to follow the conversation. You already have information from the first question sequence. Now you have to answer the question," <u>What</u> do you like to <u>do</u> on weekends?", and give a question to continue.

Sally: I <u>look</u> on the internet for movies and concerts. <u>What</u> do you like to do? Medicine has a lot of homework.

Sally answers the question with equal information and asks the same question in return. This circle of returning questions.

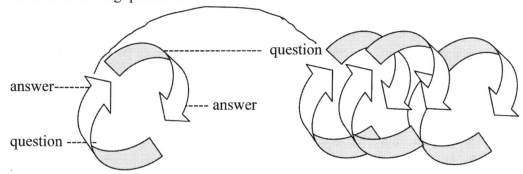

Now you can see how conversation works. Using one word answers do not make a conversation. Using short questions that do not ask for information make conversation boring.

In this conversation you will find very few one word answers. "Do, Are, Is, Was" questions will always get one word answers and not much information. Using them in conversation is ok once in a while. If you use them too much the conversation will not give you any information just a lot more questions. If you like to answer questions or ask a lot of questions this is great. If you want a smoother more enjoyable conversation learn to ask better questions. With better questions you will have better conversations.

A rule of thumb in English.

Longer is better, when writing a note or asking for information get the most information. Too short and you miss good information and then have bad communication.

Sally makes a comment about the information that John had told her.

<u>Medicine has a lot of homework.</u>

Making comments about the information someone has given shows interest in the conversation. If you make comments about other ideas not related to the conversation ask a question to change the topic after the comment.

You have made several questions. Now ask them to a partner. When the partner asks the second question make a comment and ask a question to keep the topic going.

Look at the following conversation between John and Sally. You can build vocabulary by replacing the words that are numbered in each chapter. Build vocabulary through replacement of similar word ideas. This could be like "running" to "jumping". From "touching" to "choosing", if you are shopping.

Be careful of talking, speaking, saying. For these add words like talking about – speaking to, is saying. This will help with ideas like watching movies, not seeing movies.

✳ ✳ ✳ In the conversation template you will find two sets of numbers. One set will be consecutive 1-100, while the second will be only 1-10.

The 1-100 set is for every sequence of Question – Answer – Question. There are 10 of these per chapter totalling 100.

The 1-10 set are words that were used in the text chapter. There will be 10 per chapter. They are topic oriented words. Please change them to expand your vocabulary, or change the topic and then match the vocabulary to it.

CHAPTER 1
What do you like to do?

John: It's raining again. I hate rain. Oh hi! I was just speaking out loud. My name is John. I am a student. Do you live around here?[1]

Sally: No! I am new here. I don't like rain either. I'm a student at NamSeoul University. I haven't seen you before. I'm Sally. <u>Where</u> do you go to school?

John: I go to NamSeoul too. I am majoring in Medicine. <u>What</u> do you like to <u>do</u> on weekends?[2]

Sally: I <u>look</u> on the internet for movies and concerts. <u>What</u> do you like to do? Medicine has a lot of homework.

John: Yes it does, but I like sports. Sally! <u>What</u> kind of <u>movies</u> or <u>concerts</u> do you like to go to?[3]

Sally: I like <u>romantic</u> movies or <u>jazz</u> concerts. <u>Have you ever</u> been to a jazz concert?

John: Only once or twice. I guess you don't watch sports often. <u>What do you study</u> at NamSeoul?[4]

Sally: I <u>study</u> Engineering Design. I'm a freshman this year. This is basketball season, which Korean team do you <u>watch</u> the most?

John: I <u>watch</u> the <u>Samsung Kings</u>. They have won the championship the last three years. I go almost every Saturday afternoon. I take a break from my homework. I think there is a romantic movie this weekend playing at the CGV. Who is your favorite actor?[5]

Sally: I have gone to the COEX CGV, but it's always too busy. I go to the smaller ones. There are not so many people, so it is more comfortable. <u>Who is</u> <u>playing</u> in the movie? I like Channing Tatum.

John: <u>I'm not sure</u>, I didn't look. The title was **Dear John.** The poster looked quite romantic. I used to go to movies more but now I prefer sports. There are some jazz concerts every weekend. <u>Where do you like to go</u> for Jazz concerts?[6]

Sally: I usually <u>go</u> to **All that Jazz Club** or to some small Clubs close to Sookmyung Women's University. There are many small concerts there and you can see a lot of new groups. Who do you <u>go with</u>   when you go to your weekend games?

John: I usually <u>go with</u> a couple guys who live close enough to meet at the stadium. We buy seats in the middle price so we can see the players. The cheap tickets are too far way. If you sit in the middle you can see all of the game very easy. If you sit at the end it is more exciting. Who is <u>your favorite</u> Jazz musician or singer?[7]

Sally: My <u>favorite singer</u> is Annie Ross. She sings in a few comedies and goes on tour sometimes. I hope I can see her sometime. How about American sports! What <u>do you think of</u> Lebron James?

John: <u>James is a great player</u>. He is very young to play in the NBA. Maybe a future Jordon! Better than Korean sports for sure. I should get going! My mother will be waiting! How about <u>meeting</u> again?[8] I'll introduce you to more people.

Sally: <u>Sounds great</u>! Where should we meet?

John: Well, how about <u>at the mall</u>?[9] It's close and easy to get to.

Sally; <u>Ok!</u> Where in the Mall?

John: Ok! Next week at 10 at Starbucks?[10]

Sally: Fantastic! Starbucks! See you then! Bye.

CHAPTER 2
Commands

At Square Bucks Coffee wondering where Sally is…..

John: My coffee is almost finished. Oh! Sally! I was wondering if you were coming. <u>Did</u> you have a hard time finding this place?

Sally: <u>Yes</u>! But just a little bit. I hope you didn't have to wait too long. What are we going to do today?[11]

John: Wow! Look at those fish![1] <u>Aren't they big</u>?

Sally; <u>Yes! They</u> are huge! What kind of <u>fish are they</u>?[12]

John: <u>I think they</u> are giant squid! Let's ask the person over there! <u>Is</u> she the helper?

Sally: <u>Yes</u>! Hello! <u>Could</u> you help us?[13] We <u>would like</u> to know the name of those big fish over there.

John: I told her they were squid. <u>Are</u> there more fish we could see?

Helper: Well, there are lots of bigger ones. Sign the guest book first![2]

Sally: Ok! I have a pencil. Is that ok?[14]

John: Wait![3] I have a pen in my pocket. What <u>color</u> pen do you need?

Helper: Use <u>black</u> pen only![4]

Sally: Ok! What other information do you need?[15]

Helper: <u>Underline</u> why you are coming from the list![5]

John: Ok! Just to see big fish! <u>Can we go</u> anywhere with this pass?

Helper: <u>Yes! You can go</u> anywhere on this floor.

Sally: Wow! Excuse me![1] Where can we find the blue whale?[16]

Helper: I'm sorry![2] <u>Did</u> you say blue whale?

John: <u>Yes!</u> We wanted see the BIG fish! What <u>big fish</u> do you have?[17]

Helper: We don't have blue whales, but we do have <u>killer whales</u>. Sit over there[6], please!

Sally: I hate waiting. Do you know how long we have to wait?

John: Be patient! Come![7] Watch[8] the small ones! You like the small bright colored ones don't you?[18]

Sally: Yes! They are cute. Cross this out[9] as a place to go for fun. Are you having fun, John?

John: A little. It is relaxing to see new things. Isn't it better than a coffee shop with loud music?[19]

Loudspeaker: Come to the[10] front gate to see the killer whale show!

Sally: Does that mean us?

John: I think so. What should we do after the show? [20]

Sally: Maybe coffee in a nice quiet place would be good.

John: The **Nuts for English Coffee** shop looks like an interesting place.

CHAPTER 3

What's in your Bag?

Sally: Wow! Such a nice place! Everything is English. Even the wallpaper! Let's sit at this table. It has two lamps.

John: Did you see the book names on the shelves? [21]

Sally: No! Did you?

John: A few! There are some classics. Did you order already? [22]

Sally: No! Not yet! I was looking in my bag for my wallet. Did you bring some money?

John: Yes! I can pay for the coffee. Would you like a piece of cheesecake? [23]

Sally: Sounds like a good plan. Do you have your notebook in your bag? It looks heavy today.

John: Yes! I was going to work on my homework. Do you ever do homework in coffee shops? [24]

Sally: Yes! I carry my flash memory everywhere. Would you like me to show you my homework?

John: Sure! Is it English homework? [25]

Sally: Yes! Let's see if I can find it. Do you have just stuff in your bag?

John: Wow! You have a lot of lipstick in your purse. There is also a dictionary, gum and a pair of sunglasses. Yes! I have some stuff but not as much as you. Why do you have so much? [26]

Sally: Just girls stuff. What stuff you have in your bag?

John: In my backpack I have…. let's see .. my iPod, a bottle of water, pencils, and eraser. There is also a camera and a folder for printed homework. Is there a second floor in this shop?[27]

Sally: I think so! There are stairs around the corner. Would you like to go up there?

John: Sure! Oh there is only one table here! Did you want me to start my computer for you? [28] Then you can show me your file on your flash stick.

Sally: Would you? I have to make this conversation every week. It is so hard. I thought we could practice it here. Would you like to do it with me?

John: I think that would be great! Do you want me to use expression? [29]

Sally: Of course! What good is conversation without expression?

John: You are right! Conversation without expression is very boring. How can we learn good expression? [30] I've tried but it hasn't been easy.

Sally: Well! The Professor suggested we listen to radio talk shows. It is really hard because I can't hear the words well. Have you ever tried it?

John: I don't listen to radio much, but it sounds like a good idea. I usually listen to music on my MP3 player. Is your iPod full of music or talk shows?

Sally: Music of course. I do try to listen to talk shows every night though. I'm finished my coffee and the time to get back to do homework is here again. Thanks for helping me with my homework. Shall we meet next weekend, or maybe in school?

John: Sounds good! Let's try to meet here next week.

CHAPTER 4
What do you have scheduled?

Sally wakes up on Saturday but thinks it is a school day.

Sally: Oh no! It is already 9:30 in the morning [1]. Why didn't I hear the alarm clock?

Rrrrring rrrrrrring

Sally: Hello! I am so late for school my teacher will be very angry.

John: Oh Sally! It's Saturday! There is no school today, so relax. Did you forget we were going to meet today?[31]

Sally: I didn't forget! What's your **schedule** for today?

John: Well! When will you eat **breakfast**?[32]

Sally: I think I will skip breakfast this morning. Have you already had your b**reakfast**?

John: Yes! I usually have breakfast at 20 past seven [2]. (7:20). The early bird gets the worm you know. So how about lunch? [33]

Sally: I have to clean my room so I will be free after ten thirty $_3$. (10:30) Do you have **chores** to do, like cleaning your room? I have new furniture now so I have to organize my room a bit.

John: I do the dishes for my mother. She is very busy with her job so it helps. What **chores** do you do?[34]

Sally: I clean my room mostly. Sometimes I wash clothes or dishes. Do you surf the internet every day?

John: Yes! I surf the internet in the evening $_4$ from 7~10. That is when most of my friends come on and we do our homework together. Why not join us? [35] We use naver.com.

Sally: Sounds like a great idea! I study English usually at that time. I go to a private school to help me with my homework. Maybe there is another time we can meet online. What is your **schedule** after your chores?

John: I was going to share a burger with you! If you don't have breakfast maybe we could go for pizza. Would you like that? [36] In the afternoon $_5$ I will play a game of basketball at the school gym.

Sally: I'd love to have pizza! <u>When</u> is the game?

John: It is from 2:30 to about 4 o'clock $_6$. Why not be our <u>cheerleader</u>? [37]

Sally: Ha! Ha! Ok! Should I <u>wave my hands</u> and <u>shout</u> so you can play better?

John: Sounds like you have been watching TV sports. In the evening $_7$ I watch sports <u>on weekends</u>. The best games are played on weekends$_8$. What do you watch on TV <u>on the weekend</u>? [38]

Sally: I watch dramas. Sometimes they have good movies as well. Maybe I will have to watch some sports, but playing is more fun. What do you do <u>on Sunday $_9$</u>?

John: <u>On Sunday </u>I like to relax. Which Church do you go to? [39]

Sally: There is a Presbyterian Church close to my house. They have a service at 10:00 in the morning. We usually go out for lunch after. Why don't you come sometime?

John: Well! I'm not a church person. Can I meet the preacher sometime during the week? $_{40}$

Sally: I think he would like that. Let's make time in our **schedule** to meet him next week.

John: Ok! Now hurry and let's go for pizza! I'm hungry.

CHAPTER 5
Family pictures

Sally: John? Tell me about your family. Do you have any pictures of them in your wallet? 41

John: Well I have a few pictures. Family is important to me. Here is a picture of my younger brother. Do you have any pictures?

Sally: Let me see! Oh here is one of my mother? Your brother looks very handsome. How many years younger <u>is he</u>¹? 42

John: He is 8 years younger than me. Some people think we from different families. <u>He is</u>² very different than me. Do you want some more coffee?

Sally: Sure! Thanks! Here is another picture. <u>She is</u>³ my sister. <u>She is</u> 4 years older than me. Oh! <u>Who is</u>⁴ that in that picture? 43 There are so many people in it.

John: Oh that one! That is a picture of my family. My father is very funny. He likes to have these big pictures. I don't see my brother much but they are all very friendly. <u>What are</u>⁵ your parents like?

Sally: My mother is a good cook. <u>She is</u> 85 years old. <u>What is</u>⁶ your brother like? 44 You said <u>he is</u> different than you.

John: He is an artist. He likes to draw cartoons of everybody. When you meet him you will have to ask him to draw one for you. Do you have any brothers or sisters?

Sally: I have an older brother. <u>His name is</u>⁷ Hank. He is hardworking and serious. Do you have any more pictures? 45

John: Oh! <u>Who is this</u>⁸ picture of? It looks like a younger you.

Sally: That is my sister. We are very close to each other. Many people think we are the same. <u>She is</u> really outgoing. Do you have any sisters? 46

John: I do but she is older than me. She works in a school. She is a teacher's helper. What does your sister do?

Sally: My <u>sister is</u>⁹ a working mother. She has a small girl. <u>It is</u> hard sometimes, but she will do ok. Being a young mother can be tough sometimes. Do you have any grandparents? 48

John: Yes! I have grandparents. They live in Vancouver. <u>They are</u>¹⁰ very kind and always do special things when we visit?

Sally: Wow! Sounds like you have a good time there. My grandparents are good sports fans. They go to the soccer stadium every weekend. Does your family do anything special for Easter? 49

John: No! Sometimes we go to church. It is a family tradition. The children make eggs and my parents buy candy eggs to enjoy. What does your family do for Easter?

Sally: We go to church of course. Easter is not about eggs and bunnies. It is about Jesus rising from the dead. We sing special songs and have a special choir. Are you traveling this Easter holiday to see your grandparents? 50

John: No this year my brother has to take a test and my sister is too busy. So this year we will stay here. Maybe we can meet at the Mall for an Easter treat. Would you like that?

Sally: Sounds great! Let's make a plan. I'll call you.

John: Ok! Later! Bye.

CHAPTER 6
Shopping for Clothes

Sally has looked in her wardrobe and found that many of her clothes are missing buttons, and not looking so pretty anymore. Summer is coming and ……

Sally: Hey Mom?! Could you give me some money to buy some new clothes?

Mom: Sally! You have lots of clothes!

Sally: I know but many of them are missing buttons and don't fit anymore.

Mom: Ok! Ask me on Friday so I don't forget.

Sally: Ok.

~~~~~   Sally goes to her room to phone John.   ~~~~~

Sally: Hey John! What are doing on Saturday? 51

John: Not much on Saturday! What do you have planned?

Sally: I'm going clothes shopping. I need to get some <u>T-shirts</u> [1], a <u>jacket</u> [2], new <u>shoes</u> [3], and maybe a new <u>sweater</u> [4]. Would you like to   come? [52]

John: Sounds great! The new styles are very bright, with lots of <u>polka dots</u> [5] and <u>flowers</u> [6]. What color are you looking for?

Sally: I like <u>yellow stripes</u> [7] or <u>flower patterns</u> [8]. Do you need anything for spring or summer? [53]

John: I might get some <u>jeans</u> or <u>shorts</u>. Usually the <u>brand</u> I like is very <u>expensive</u>. Do you buy name brand stuff?

Sally: No! Usually just what is on sale. They are usually good quality but last year's style. I like <u>cotton</u> [9] for summer. What jean brand do you buy?[54]

John: I like Levi's. They last for a long time. Their denim [10] is heavier than other <u>cheap</u>er brands. How about meeting at the Mall in an hour?

Sally: Ok! I'll be there.

~~~ At the Mall shopping ~~~

John: Hey there is a sale over there! How much are these?

Sales Lady: Those are sixty-nine ninety-five!

John: Is there a different color? I like black better than green.

Sales Lady: Yes! What style would you like? [55]

John: Relaxed fit if you have it! Did you see anything Sally? There are some t-shirts on sale over there.

Sally: Wow! A really big sale! I like these striped ones. How much are they?[56]

Sales Lady: Those are five for 15 dollars. What size do you need? You look like a size 95.

Sally: Right! I'm a size ninety-five. Are there more sizes with the green and orange stripes? [57] I can only find two!

John: I found a leather jacket for Spring. I have been looking for this style for a long time. The sales lady said it's on sale for one hundred fifty dollars. Did you find anything else? You were looking for sweaters.

Sally: They don't have nice sweaters in this store. I will have to go to Galleria. The best and newest fashions are found there. I saw a lot of flowered sweaters there last week. Do you have time to go there today? [58]

John: Sure! I have lots of time today! Maybe I can find some shorts there. Aren't they a bit expensive?

Sally: Well… that is true but I think I will buy only one sweater. Why not get a pair of those new safari shorts? [59]

John: My mom would never let <u>spend</u> that much money on a pair of shorts. What will your mom say if you spend that much money?

Sally: You are right! I should not spend so much on one when I can buy more. Where should we go for new sweaters? [60]

John: I think LotteMart is a good start. Let's go look and then your mother will be happy. If she is happy you will be happy. Right?

Sally: What a great idea. You are right.

     *** Sally and John go to LotteMart and then home to see what her mother will say.

CHAPTER 7
What do you do on weekends?

Mom: Wow! How much money did you spend?

Sally: Well…. Not all of it, just most of it. I'm not sure that next weekend I will go shopping. I need to clean my room <u>more often</u> [1]. Hey John! Do you <u>often</u> do things with your family on weekends? [61]

John: Well, my family is quite busy. We <u>often</u> don't do activities together. We do things by ourselves or with another family member, like my sister and I will <u>play tennis</u> on Saturday. Do you always do things as a family?

Sally: No! Not <u>always</u> [2]. If there is a special occasion we will <u>go on a picnic</u> to the mountain. It is close and it doesn't take a lot of work. How often do you <u>go on picnics</u> with your family? [62]

John: We <u>never</u> [3] go on picnics. We went to the mountain once. It was a school trip. <u>Most</u> [4] <u>weekends</u> my father is not home. He works out of town. I also play sports, so I <u>almost always</u> have a game on weekends. What about your brother? What does he do on weekends?

Sally: My brother? He has band practice. He is <u>usually</u> [5] making a lot of noise in the house practicing. What about your sister? What does she usually do on weekends? [63]

John: My sister is <u>usually</u> practicing English on the computer. She listens to npr.org and then writes the ideas she hears. She usually sleeps until noon on Saturday. She is very lazy. When do you <u>do your homework</u> on weekends? I never have time.

Sally: <u>Sometimes</u> [6] I do my homework late at night. Then I sleep in. Have you ever handed your homework in late? [64] My teacher takes points off if it is late.

John: I <u>hardly ever</u> [7] hand my work in late. I try <u>to do my homework</u> on weekdays. Do you want to <u>go to the movies</u> on Friday night?

Sally: I'm sorry. This weekend I will <u>go out to a restaurant</u> with my Uncle's family. What about Saturday to the Matinee? [65]

John: I <u>never</u> [8] <u>go to the Matinee shows</u>. I thought they were just for kids. How about in the evening? Would you like to <u>go singing</u> in a karaoke room?

Sally: Sounds like an interesting idea. How often do you go to the karaoke room on weekends? [66]

John: It would be my first time. I <u>go dancing</u> <u>sometimes</u> [9] on Sundays in the evening. Do you like dancing?

Sally: Sunday night! This weekend I will <u>go shopping</u> with my cousins. I like the idea. I am not very good <u>at dancing</u>. I need to hold on to you very tight. Sunday is <u>usually</u> my night to relax, but we could try it sometime. Mondays I have an early class. When do you relax on weekends? [67]

John: I never have time on weekends. If I don't do things with you I play basketball. Sometimes I <u>play</u> <u>cards</u> with my friends. We do that <u>usually</u> when it rains and we can't play outside. Do you <u>play games</u> on rainy days?

Sally: Yes! I <u>often</u> <u>play</u> board <u>games</u> with my mom. She is good at them and beats me <u>all</u> [10] the time. How often do you win? [68]

John: I don't often win, but it is fun. Have you listened to the new music group 2PM?

Sally: No! Most of the time I listen to the older romantic songs. Do you download new songs to your MP3? [69]

John: Yes! Some weekends I have time so I usually try to download a few new ones. Have you ever tried doing that?

Sally: No! I have <u>never</u> had success in doing that. I don't have an MP3 either. How about just coffee today? This weekend seems to be so full of activities.

John: Ok! I think the schedule next week is not so busy. Call me on Friday!

Sally: Ok.

CHAPTER 8
Let's eat

Friday Sally hasn't seen John all week. It just seemed he was very busy. Her teacher had asked her to make a party for some foreign teachers. They were from South Korea. She really needed some help. Finally on Friday she called John.

Sally: Oh John! I don't know what to do! I have to plan a party for some foreigners from South Korea. Do you know what they eat? [70]

John: They eat a lot of rice. Do you have any rice?

Sally: I don't have any [1] rice! I guess I will have to go shopping. What do you think I need? [71]

John: Well, let's think a little. How many onions do you have?

Sally: I have a few [2] onions. I don't think I need any more. What about bananas? Do they eat bananas? [73]

John: Yes! That sounds good. How many [3] do you have?

Sally: I have lots of [4] bananas. I think we should get several [5] bags of chips. Why not come shopping with me? [74] It won't take too long.

John: Sure! I'll be right over!

John and Sally go shopping at the grocery store on the corner.

Sally: Excuse me! Do you have any fresh whole chickens? [75]

John: They are over here! Each one is about 1 kgs. Do you think we should get a few [6] apples?

Sally: We can make a fruit salad. I heard they like apples. I don't have much milk though. I need to get some [7]. How about sugar or sweets? [76] I know they like it in their coffee. They call it milk coffee. John: A sweet potato cake would be good for dessert. They only have a few[8] here. Don't you think we need fish? They are Korean and fish is a normal food for them.

Sally: What a great thinker you are! We need a head of cabbage as well and <u>some</u> ₉ mayo. Do you think cabbage and mayo go well together? [77]

John: I saw some instant noodles. South Korea is famous for them. <u>How many</u> should I buy?

Sally: Why not buy a dozen! What kinds of noodles are there? [78] Usually there are <u>several</u> ₁₀ different flavors.

John: Don't forget the green tea, a South Korean favorite. I didn't see <u>any</u>. Is it close to where you are?

Sally: Well I think we bought enough to last for a day. It will be <u>a lot of</u> hard work. Oh! Did you bring your wallet? [79] I can't find mine in my purse.

John: I have a <u>few</u> dollars but I'm not sure I have enough. <u>How much</u> do you need?

Sally: I need about 45 dollars. I feel silly. Do you have that much? [80]

John: I have 46 dollars. Just enough! How are you going to get home? I think it is too far, and there are too <u>many</u> groceries.

Sally: I was hoping you would help carry them. Would you do that for me?

John: It would be a pleasure. Since we came in the car it will easy to take you home.

Sally: Thank you so much!

CHAPTER 9
Where have you been?

Sally: "I'm so tired. This party takes too much time. I need to take a trip!"

*** Sally was wondering where she would go. The South Korean teachers were coming and John had said he had been in a school overseas. Just then the telephone rang.

Sally: Hello! John! I am so excited. I need to ask you some questions. Would you give me some good answers? [81]

John: Sure! Ask me and I will answer. This party must have made your brain crazy. What would you like to know?

Sally: I would like to know if you have any friends in another country. Maybe even an uncle or aunt. Do you have any? [82] Mine are living in different cities but not countries. I thought it would be fun to see what they <u>are doing</u>.

John : Sounds like fun. I think I have some phone numbers of some friends. I have an uncle in Africa. I think they are about 7 hours ahead of us, so we need to phone them at 10 in the morning. I'll come over and we can phone them. Is that ok with you?

Sally: Sounds great! What country are they in? [83]

John arrives at Sally's house and they get ready to phone.

John: They live in Mali. They write letters all the time. They have four children. Are you ready? Let's do it!

They connect to the Uncle in Africa

John: Uncle George! <u>What are you doing now</u> $_1$? [84]

Uncle George: I am preparing to go on a trip to Timbuktu. <u>Have you ever been there</u>?

John: No, but it sounds like fun. How's Jamie? <u>What is she doing now</u> $_2$? [85]

Uncle George: Jamie <u>is hanging out</u> $_3$ with her friends. She is very popular. What are you doing?

John: I am with my friend Sally. We go to the same school. Do you want to talk with her? [86]

Uncle George: Sounds great! June, our youngest <u>is riding a camel</u> $_4$. Would she like to ride a camel?

John: I think so. Let me give the phone to her.

Sally: Mr. Sim! Riding a camel sounds like fun. I like riding horses. What are your other children doing? [87]

Uncle George: Well, <u>Julie is playing soccer</u> $_5$. He will come home at 5 o'clock in the afternoon. John likes sports. Do you like sports?

Sally: What about the others? What are their names and what are they doing? [88]

Uncle George: The other two children's names are Jackie and Juno. Jackie <u>is practicing</u> $_6$ tae kwon do. Juno <u>is watching TV</u> $_7$. Why not visit us sometime?

Sally: I'd love to. What TV programs can you watch in Africa? [89]

Uncle George: We watch CSI most of the time. What are you doing today?

Sally: George and I <u>are going</u> ₈ to a great hamburger place, Michelle's the Queen of Burgers. It is our favorite place to eat. What is your wife doing? ⁹⁰

Uncle George: <u>She is eating</u> ₉ a piece of fresh apple pie. It is the season for apples here. So when are you coming here?

Sally: I won't make any promises. John! What a lovely family. How about lunch? I'm hungry.

John: Ok! It's off to Michelle's for a NamSeoul special.

CHAPTER 10
Where will I be in the future?

At Michelle's restaurant.

Sally: John? We will be finished school soon. Do you ever think about what you want to do school? ⁹¹

John: Yes! I do once in a while. I think it will take a lot of <u>hard work</u> ₁ but I want an <u>interesting job</u> ₂. What about you? What do you see in the future?

Sally: I think that in the future I want to live in another country? My teacher is from New Zealand, and she always tells us it is comfortable to live in. In your future do you think you will have to move to another country? ₉₂

John: I hope not. I want to find a nice wife and <u>have many children</u> ₃. What job do you think you will have in New Zealand?

Sally: I <u>predict</u> ₄ that I will be on TV in a short time. I think Sam and Julie want to live in South Korea. They will have to work hard to save money! Do you think that it is a good idea? ⁹³

John: Not so soon. I think they will have to get more experience first. I want to become <u>a good English speaker.</u>₅ Are you going to be famous?

Sally: I <u>plan</u> ₆ to get my Degree first. Then I want to do commercials for Samsung. Where do you think technology will be in the future? ⁹⁴

John: I think technology will be very small. <u>People will live in space</u> ₇. Can you imagine phoning your teacher in space?

Sally: Well it would be very sunny or very dark if they lived on the moon. How many years will it take to get there? [95]

John: I think it will take five more years before they get serious about it. Where will you be in five years?

Sally: This year I plan to start my Degree. I need to <u>get good grades</u> [8] so I can enter. In five years I hope to be in New Zealand. What about you? [96]

John: If I <u>am going to be</u> [9] an Engineer I will still be in school. What about in ten years?

Sally: In ten years I will <u>be rich</u> [10] because I won the lottery. The weather will be <u>hot and sunny</u> because I will live in New Zealand. Isn't ten years a long time? [97]

John: Ten years is a short time. Everything is changing faster. Soon we will have English in our DNA. We won't have to study it any more. What do you think?

Sally: Probably not, but the idea is nice. Imagine living a long life. How long would you want to live if you could choose? [98]

John: That is a good question. With technology maybe we will never have to die. What will happen to my pension?

Sally: You will never stop working, if I know you. Did you hear about the British man who is still cleaning cars at 99 years old? [99]

John: Wow! Is it possible?

Sally: Believe it or not! It is true! Well it's late again. Time flies so fast when you have fun. Imagine one semester feels so slow in the beginning but it is over so fast. Ten years is not very far. Just today it seems like forever. When can we get together again? [100]

John: Yes! It is so true. Well let's get together again. So far these weekends have been a lot of fun.

Sally: And my English is improving. See you soon John! Bye!

John: You too! Soon! Bye!